What is Pollination?

Types of Pollinators

Pollination Process

Plant Adaptations

Pollination Activities

Life Cycle of Plants

Quiz and Games

Main parts of a typical plant

Main parts of a flower

Main parts of a plant root

Main parts of a fruit

What is Pollination?

Pollination is the process by which pollen (a fine powder containing male reproductive cells) is transferred from the male part of a flower (called the anther) to the female part (called the stigma) of the same or another flower. This process is essential for the production of seeds and fruits in flowering plants.

There are two main types of pollination

Self-Pollination:

Pollen moves from the anther to the stigma of the same flower or another flower on the same plant.

Cross-Pollination:

Pollen is transferred from the anther of one plant to the stigma of a flower on a different plant of the same species. This usually results in stronger, more diverse offspring.

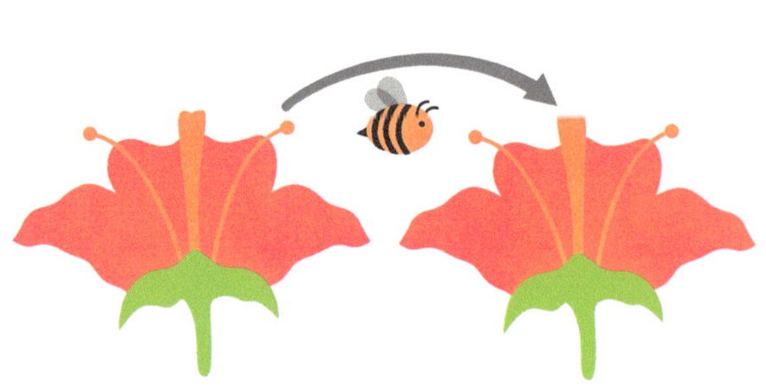

Pollination can occur through

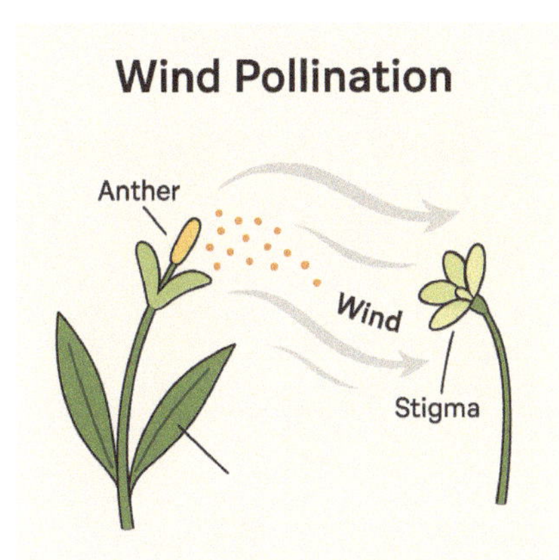

Wind pollination

Bird pollination

Insect pollination

Bats pollination

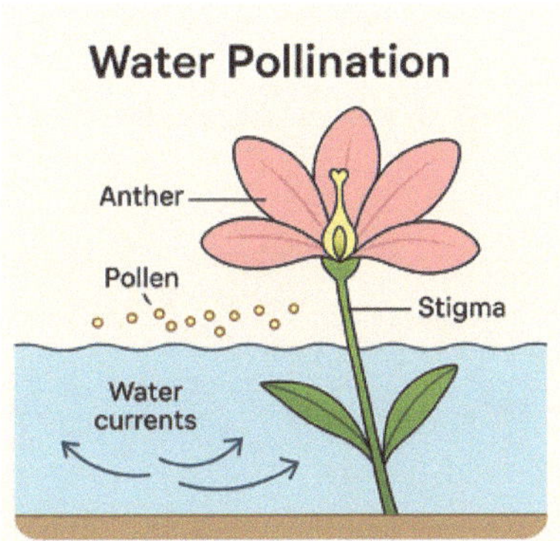

Water pollination

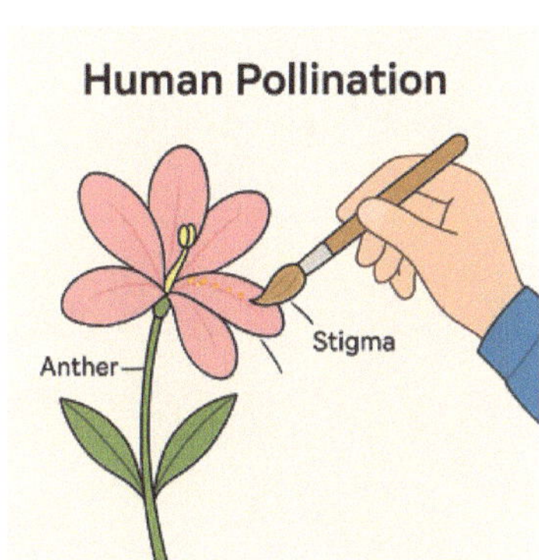

Human (in agriculture)

Self-Pollination

Self-pollination is the process where pollen grains from the anther (male part) of a flower land on the stigma (female part) of the same flower or another flower on the same plant.

💡 Key Characteristics of Self-Pollination:

Same Plant: The pollen does not travel to another plant.

Same Species: It occurs within the same flower or between flowers on the same plant.

Less Genetic Variation: Since it involves one parent plant, the offspring are usually genetically similar to the parent.

Two Types of Self-Pollination

Autogamy:

Pollen moves from the anther to the stigma of the same flower.

Example: Peas, tomatoes

Geitonogamy

Pollen is transferred from the anther of one flower to the stigma of another flower on the same plant.

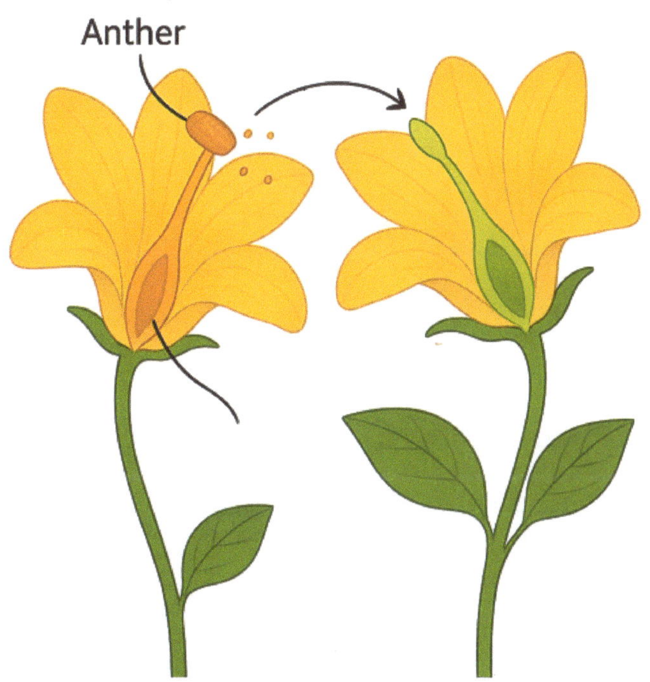

🌬️ Wind Pollination (Anemophily)

Wind pollination is the process where pollen grains are carried by the wind from the anther (male part) of one flower to the stigma (female part) of another flower — usually of the same species.

👋 How It Works:

Flowers release large amounts of pollen into the air.

Wind carries the pollen to the stigmas of nearby flowers.

No insects or animals are needed.

🌾 Characteristics of Wind-Pollinated Plants:

Small, dull-colored flowers (not showy)

No scent or nectar

Exposed stamens and stigmas for easy pollen transfer

Produce lots of lightweight pollen

Often have feathery stigmas to catch pollen from the air

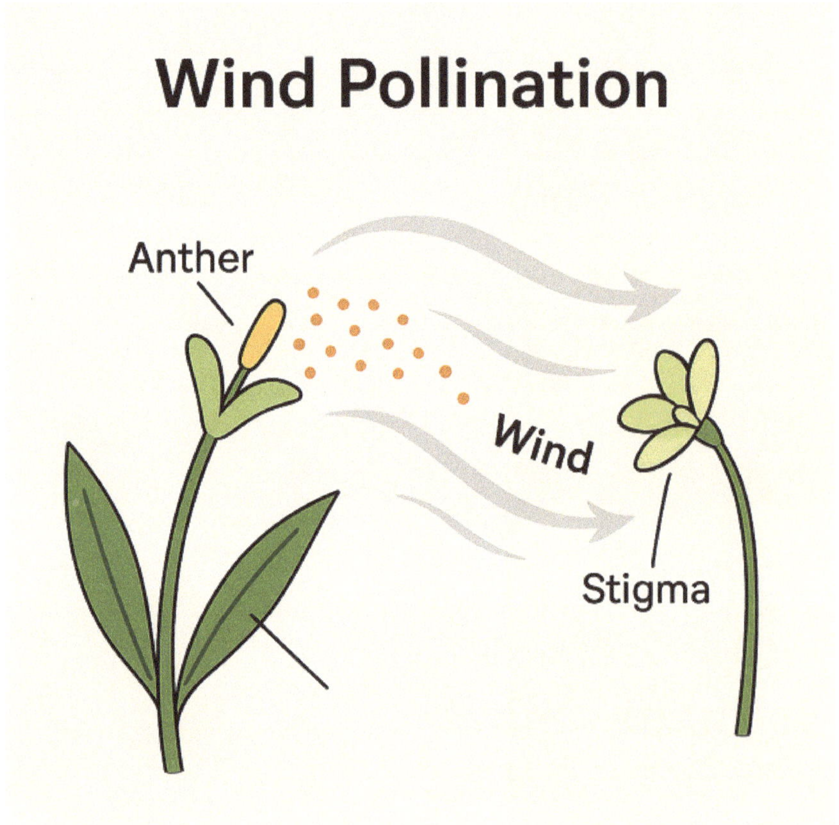

Examples of Wind-Pollinated Plants:

Grasses (e.g., wheat, rice, maize)
Trees (e.g., oak, pine, birch)
Corn
Ragweed

Advantages:

Does not rely on insects or animals
Can cover long distances

Disadvantages:

Wastes a lot of pollen
Less targeted $\rightarrow$ lower success rate
Affected by weather conditions

Bird Pollination (Ornithophily)

Bird pollination is the process where birds, especially nectar-feeding ones like hummingbirds, sunbirds, or honeyeaters, transfer pollen from the anther of one flower to the stigma of another flower while feeding on nectar.

🌸 How It Works:

- Birds are attracted to bright-colored, nectar-rich flowers.

- While sipping nectar, pollen sticks to their beaks or feathers.

- As they move to the next flower, pollen is transferred to the stigma, completing pollination.

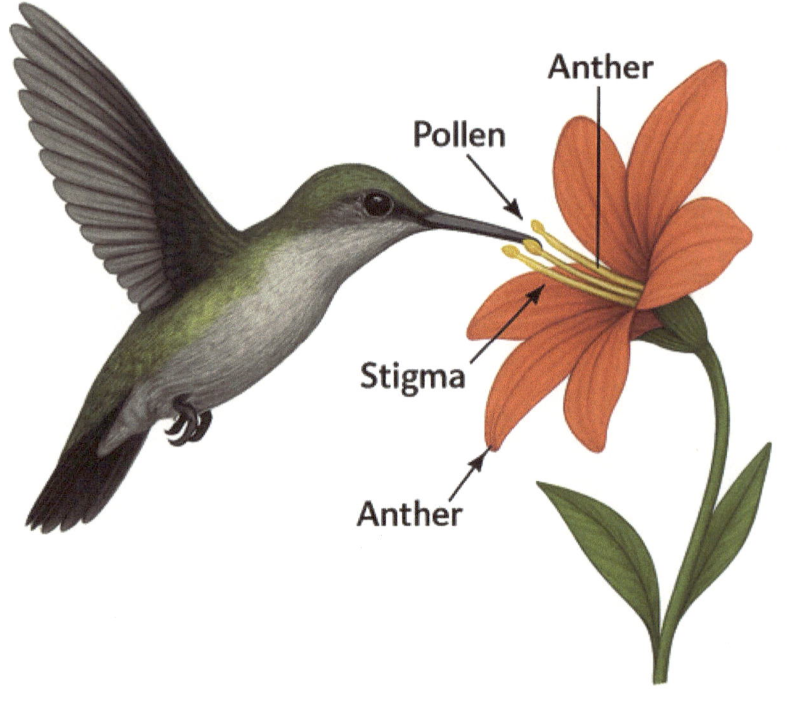

Flower Features Adapted for Bird Pollination:

Bright colors: Especially red, orange, and yellow
No scent: Birds don't rely on smell
Tubular or funnel-shaped flowers
Strong stems or hanging positions to support birds
Large nectar supply as a food reward

❧ Examples of Bird-Pollinated Plants:

Hibiscus, Fuchsia, Bottlebrush, Heliconia, Trumpet, Vine and Grevillea

Advantages:

Birds travel long distances, promoting cross-pollination
Effective even when insect pollinators are scarce
Pollination is more targeted due to the bird's feeding behavior

Disadvantages:

Plants depend on specific bird species
Birds need to be present year-round or seasonally
Flower structure must be adapted to bird access

🦇 Bat Pollination (Chiropterophily)

Bat pollination is a type of pollination where bats, mainly nectar-feeding bats, carry pollen from one flower to another while feeding at night. It's most common in tropical and desert regions.

🌷 **How It Works:**
At night, bats are attracted to large, pale-colored, and scented flowers.

As they drink nectar, pollen sticks to their fur.

When they visit another flower, the pollen rubs off on the stigma, allowing the plant to reproduce.

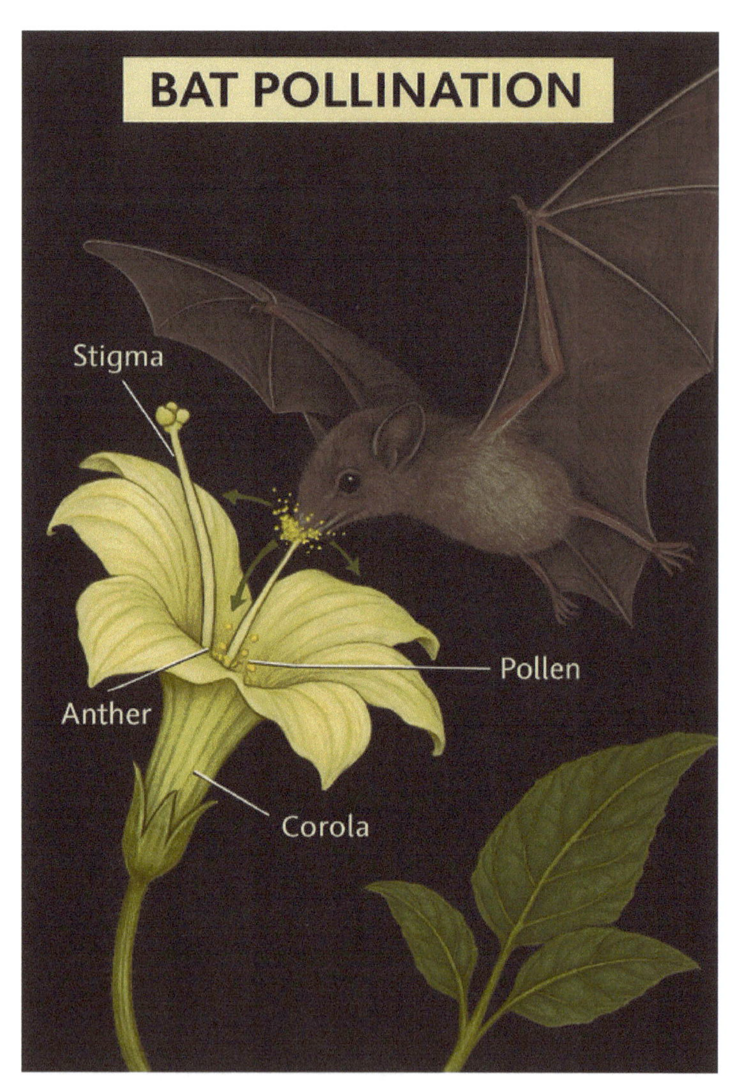

🖤 Features of Bat-Pollinated Flowers:

Open at night
White or pale-colored (easier to see in the dark)
Strong fruity or musky scent
Large and sturdy (to support bats)
Produce lots of nectar and pollen

🌿 Examples of Bat-Pollinated Plants:

Banana, Mango, Guava, Agave, sausage tree and Durian

Advantages:

Bats travel long distances, helping with cross-pollination
Pollination happens at night, when other pollinators are inactive

Disadvantages:

Flowers depend on bats being present and healthy
Not common in all regions

Water Pollination (Hydrophily)

Water pollination is a type of pollination where pollen is transferred through water from the male part (anther) of one flower to the female part (stigma) of another flower.

🏵 **How It Works:**

This happens in aquatic plants that live completely or partially in water.

Pollen is either:

Released into the water and floats to another flower, or
Carried by water currents to reach the stigma of another flower.

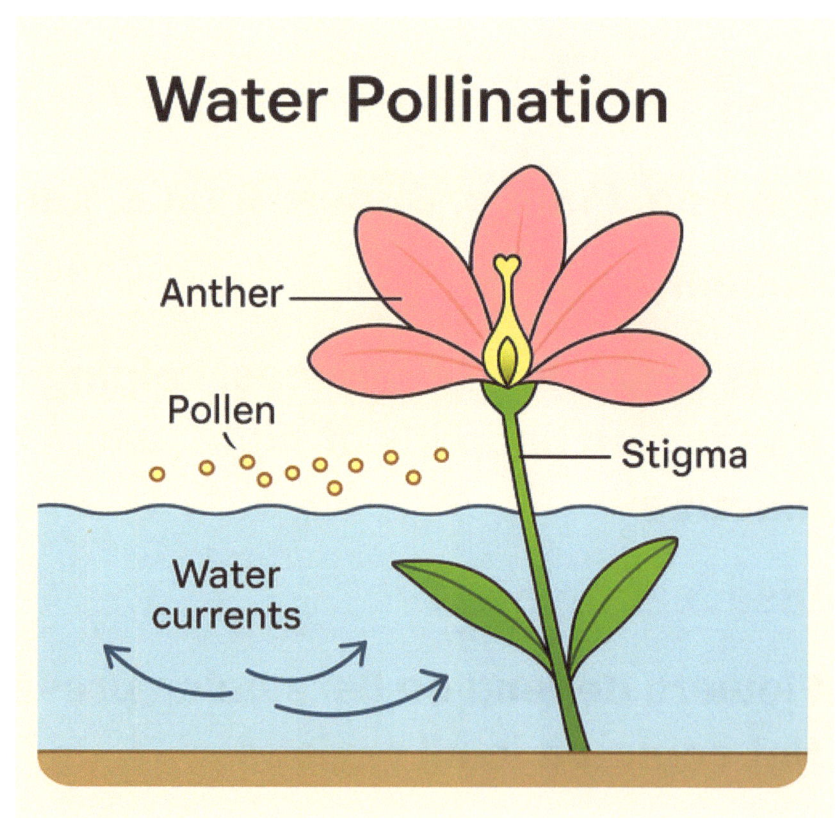

🌊 Types of Water Pollination:

Epihydrophily:

Pollen floats on the surface of the water.
Example: Vallisneria

Hypohydrophily:

Pollen travels underwater to reach the stigma.
Example: Zostera (a type of seagrass)

🌿 Examples of Water-Pollinated Plants

Vallisneria

Zostera

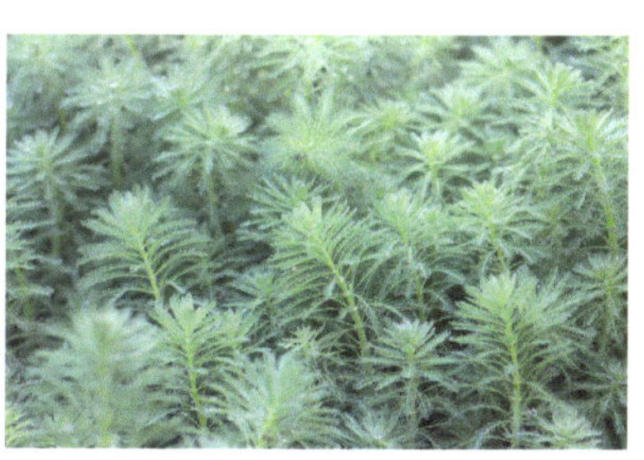

Hydrilla

Advantages:

Does not depend on pollinators like bees or wind.
Quick and efficient, especially in stable environments.
Maintains pure traits across generations.

Disadvantages:

Produces less genetic diversity.
May lead to weaker offspring over time due to inbreeding.

🐝 Insect Pollination (Entomophily)

Insect pollination is the process where insects, such as bees, butterflies, moths, beetles, and flies, transfer pollen from the anther of one flower to the stigma of another, helping plants reproduce.

🌹 How It Works:

Insects are attracted to flowers by bright colors, scents, and nectar.

As they land and feed, pollen sticks to their bodies.

When they visit the next flower, some of that pollen rubs off on the stigma, leading to fertilization.

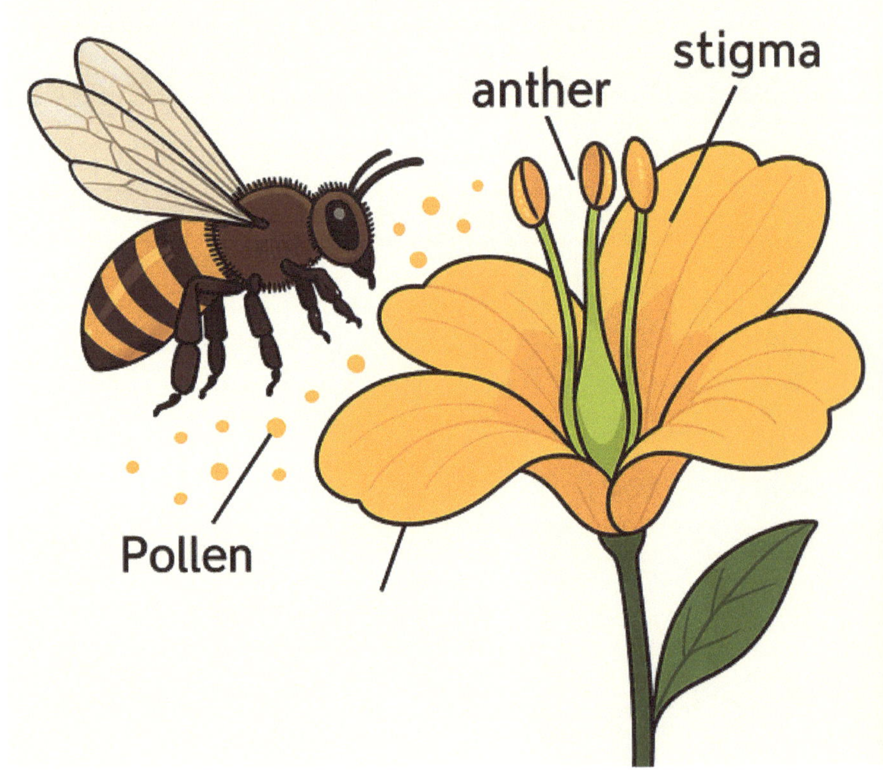

Features of Insect-Pollinated Flowers:

Brightly colored petals (especially blue, yellow, violet)
Sweet scent
Nectar as a reward
Sticky or spiky pollen that clings to insects
Smaller amounts of pollen compared to wind-pollinated flowers

 **Examples of Insect-Pollinated Plants:**

Roses, Sunflower, Daisies, Apples, Strawberries, Lavender

Advantages:

Very efficient and targeted pollination
Less pollen is wasted
Promotes genetic diversity

Disadvantages:

Depends on insect populations
Affected by climate, pesticides, and habitat loss
Some plants may fail to reproduce if pollinators are absent

Human (Artificial) Pollination in Agriculture

Human pollination, also called artificial pollination, is when humans manually transfer pollen from the anther of one flower to the stigma of another. This is done to control the breeding process, improve crop yields, or overcome a lack of natural pollinators.

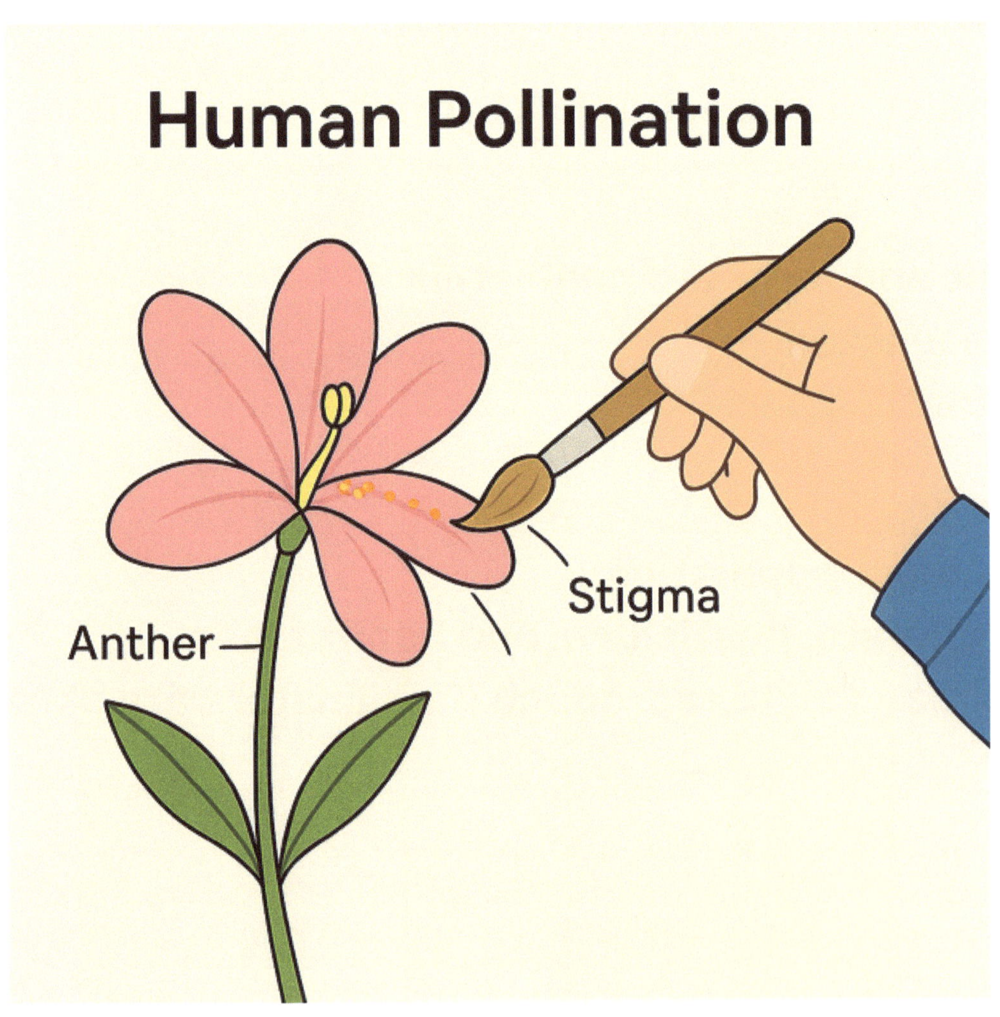

🐝 How Human Pollination Works:

Collect Pollen

Use a brush, cotton swab, or fingers to gently remove pollen from the anther of a flower.

Transfer Pollen

Apply the collected pollen to the stigma of another flower.

Repeat

Continue the process across multiple flowers to ensure pollination success

 # When Is It Used?

- Pollinators are missing (e.g., no bees due to pesticides or climate change)
- Greenhouses or indoor farming where insects can't enter
- Hybrid seed production (to control parent plants)
- To increase fruit size or shape (in crops like vanilla, watermelon, apples)

 Examples of Crops Using Human Pollination:

Vanilla orchids (naturally pollinated only by one bee species in Mexico)
Watermelons
Tomatoes (in greenhouses)
Apples and pears (in areas with low bee populations)

Benefits:

More control over which plants cross
Can happen even without insects or wind
Improves fruit quality and consistency

Drawbacks:

Labor-intensive
Expensive on a large scale
Not suitable for all crops

🌱 Plant Life Cycle – Explained Simply

🌿 1. Seed

The life of a plant begins with a seed.
Seeds contain a tiny baby plant (called an embryo) and stored food to help it grow.
Seeds need water, air, and the right temperature to sprout.

🌱 2. Germination

When the seed gets the right conditions, it germinates (sprouts).
A small root grows downward, and a shoot grows upward.
This is the beginning of growth.

🌿 3. Seedling

The young plant is called a seedling.
It grows leaves and a stem.
It uses sunlight, water, and air to make its own food through photosynthesis.

✿ 4. Adult Plant

The plant grows larger and becomes an adult.
It develops flowers, which are important for reproduction.

✿ 5. Flower and Pollination

Flowers make pollen and eggs.
Pollination happens when pollen from one flower reaches the stigma of another (by wind, insects, etc.).

🍎 6. Fruit and Seed Formation

After pollination, the flower turns into a fruit.
Inside the fruit are seeds, which can grow into new plants.

Seeds are spread by wind, water, animals, or humans.
Once they find a good place, they start the cycle again!

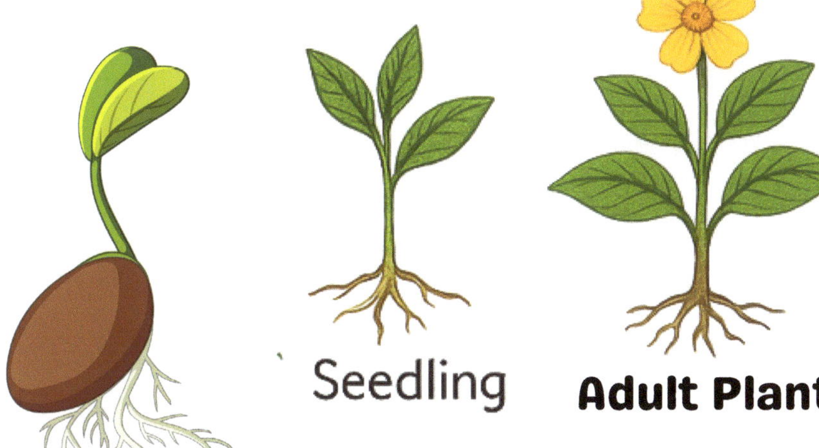

Seed

Germination

Seedling

Adult Plant

Flower and Pollination

Seed Dispersal

Fruit and Seed Formation

Main parts of a typical plant

Roots: Absorb water and nutrients, anchor the plant.

Stem: Supports the plant, transports substances.

Leaves: Perform photosynthesis, regulate water loss.

Flowers: Reproductive structures in flowering plants.

Fruits: Mature ovaries containing seeds.

Seeds: Contain genetic material for new plants.

Buds: Undeveloped shoots for new growth.

Meristems: Tissues for growth and development.

Cuticle: Waxy layer reducing water loss.

Vascular Tissues: Transport water, nutrients, and sugars.

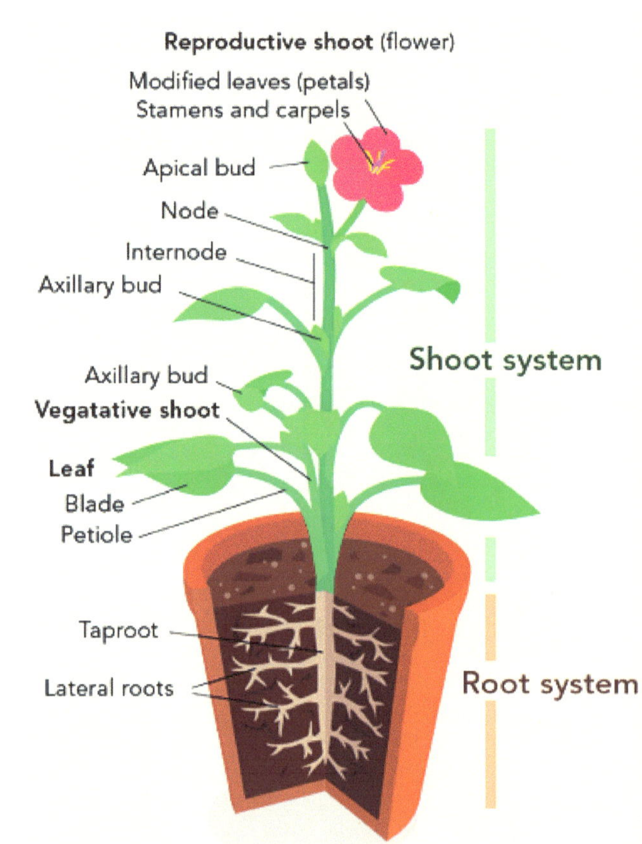

Main parts of a flower

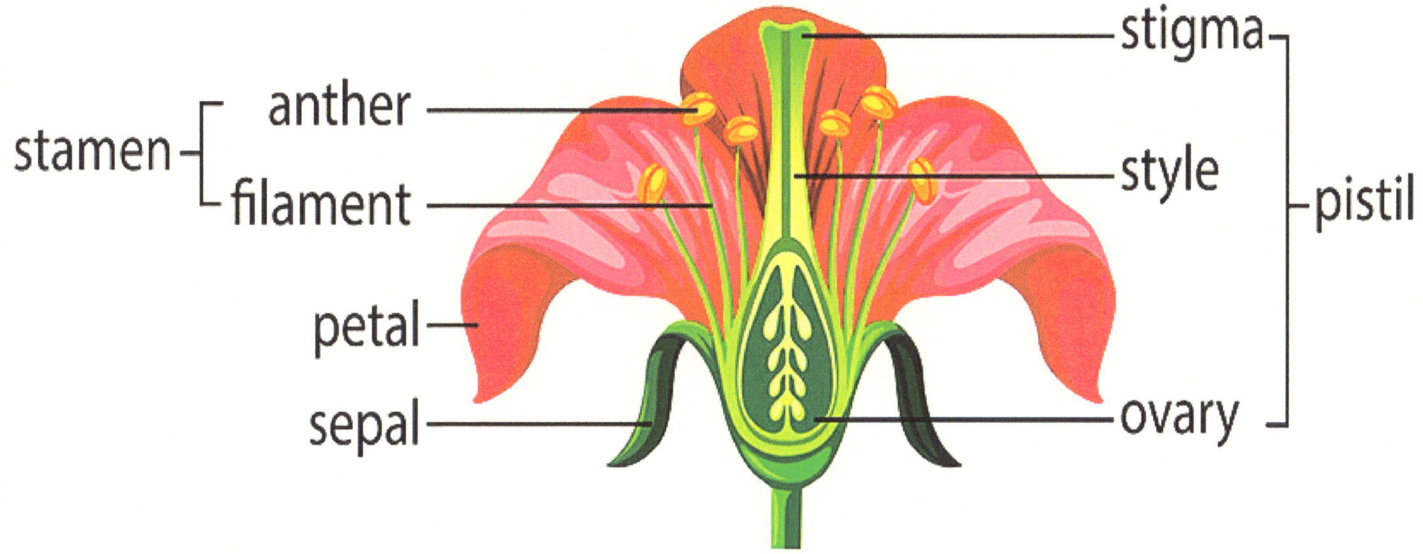

Petal: Attracts pollinators and protects reproductive organs.

Sepal: Protects the flower bud.

Stamen: The male part with the anther (holds pollen) and filament.

Pistil (Carpel): The female part with stigma (receives pollen), style, and ovary (contains ovules).

Ovule: Contains female gametes (egg cells) and becomes seeds after fertilization.

Receptacle: Supports all flower parts.

Nectary: Produces nectar to attract pollinators.

Peduncle: The stalk that connects the flower to the plant stem or branch.

Main parts of a plant root

Root Cap: Protects the tip and secretes lubricants.

Root Hairs: Tiny structures for water and nutrient absorption.

Epidermis: Outermost layer for protection.

Cortex: Stores nutrients and aids in transport.

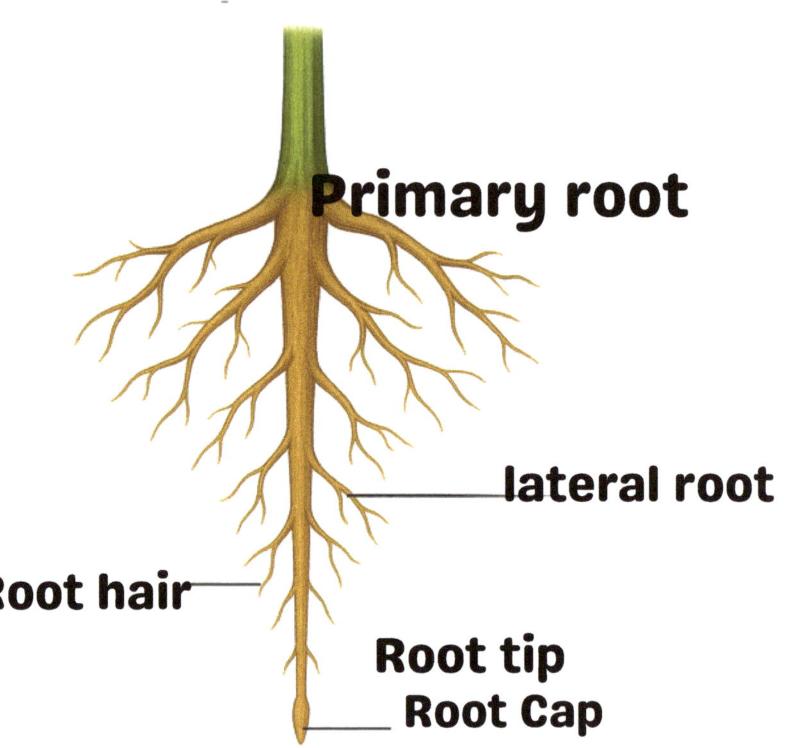

Endodermis: Regulates water and nutrient flow.

Pericycle: Gives rise to lateral roots.

Xylem and Phloem: Transport water, nutrients, and sugars.

Root Collar: Transition point to the stem/trunk.

Main parts of a fruit

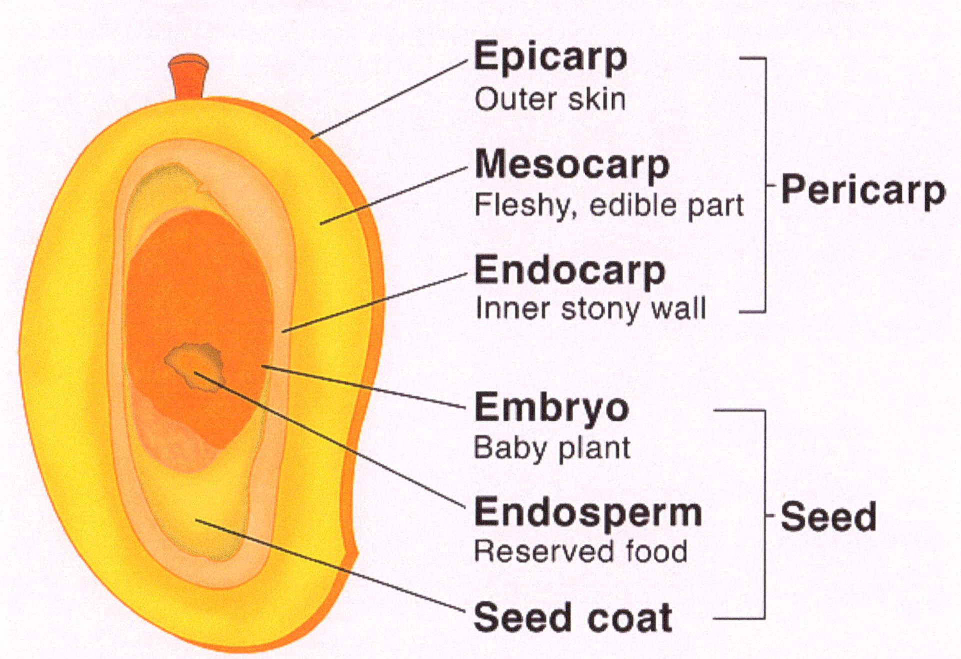

Pericarp: The outer layer with exocarp, mesocarp, and endocarp.
Seed: The reproductive structure containing an embryo.
Seed Coat: Protective covering of the seed.
Embryo: The young plant-to-be.
Endosperm: Nutrient tissue for embryo.
Carpel/Ovary Wall: Forms the fruit.
Septa: Divides some fruits into compartments.
Stem (Peduncle): Connects fruit to the plant.
Calyx: Sepals at the fruit base.
Stalk (Stipe): Connects fruit to the plant.

Main structures and components found in plant cells

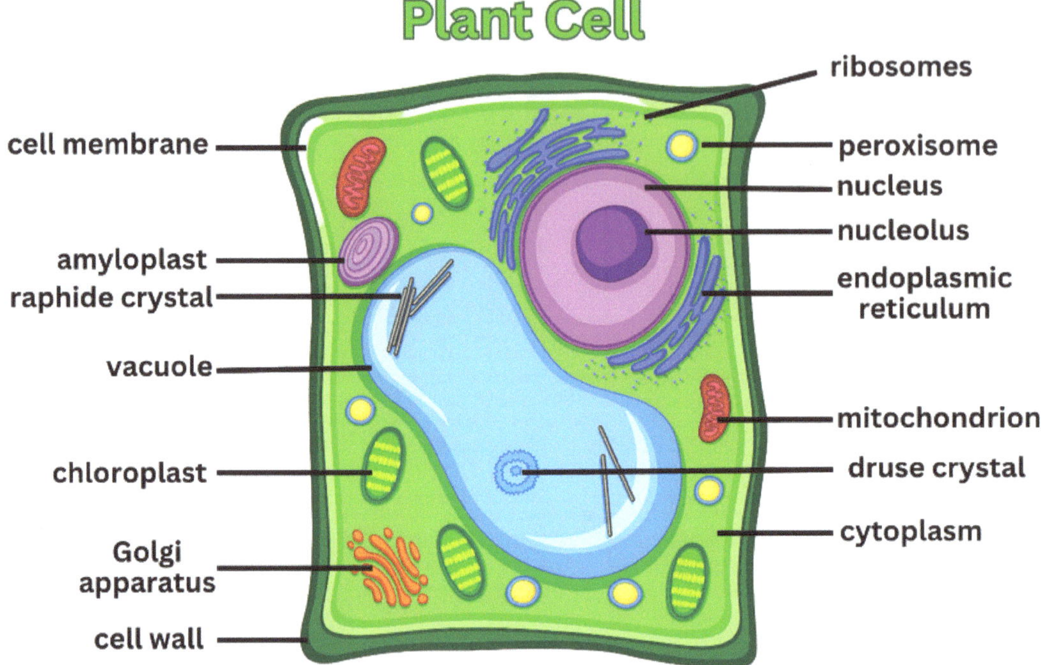

Cell Wall: Provides support and protection.

Cell Membrane: Controls substance movement.

Cytoplasm: Gel-like interior where cell processes occur.

Nucleus: Controls cell activities with DNA.

Chloroplasts: Capture sunlight for photosynthesis.

Mitochondria: Produce cell energy (ATP).

Endoplasmic Reticulum: Synthesizes proteins and lipids.

Plant Cell

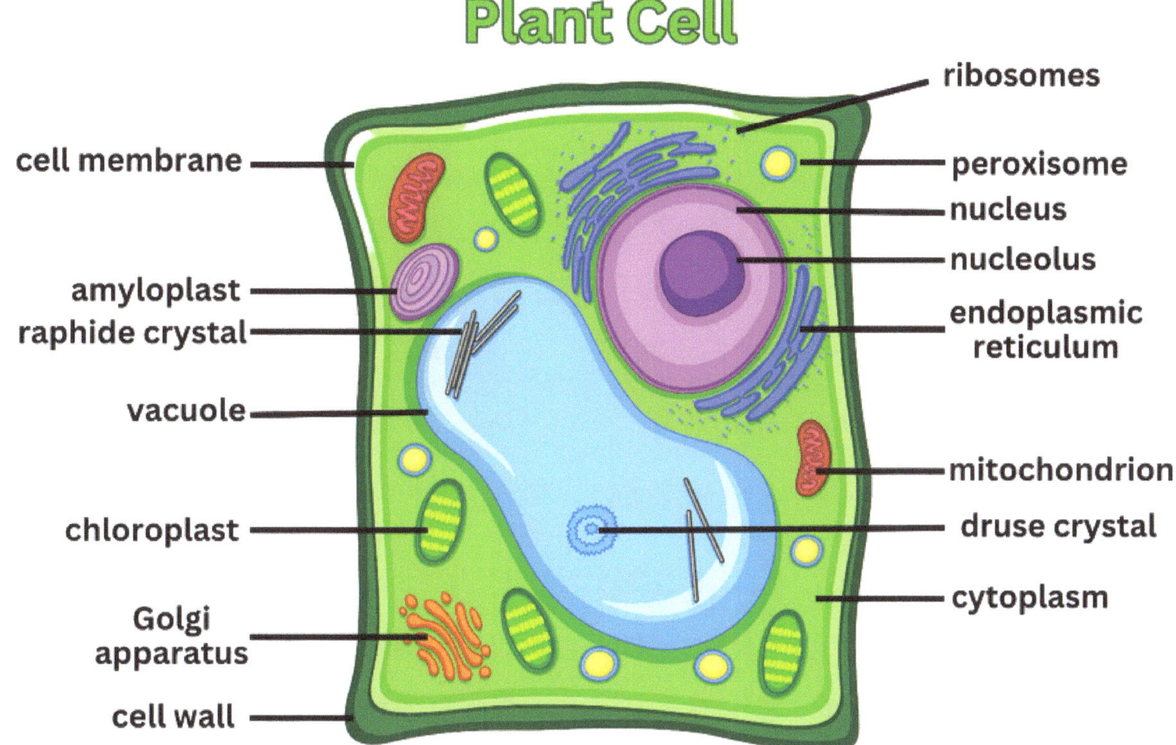

Golgi Apparatus: Packages and transports cellular products.

Vacuole: Stores water and nutrients, maintains cell shape.

Ribosomes: Produce proteins.

Cytoskeleton: Provides structure and transport pathways.

Peroxisomes: Participate in metabolic processes.

Plasmodesmata: Channels for cell communication.

Cell Wall:

The cell wall is a rigid outer layer that provides structural support and protection to the plant cell. It is made primarily of cellulose, a complex carbohydrate. The cell wall is responsible for the cell's shape and prevents it from bursting when water enters the cell.

Cell Membrane (Plasma Membrane):

The cell membrane is a phospholipid bilayer that surrounds the plant cell. It controls the movement of substances in and out of the cell and plays a role in cell communication.

Cytoplasm:

The cytoplasm is a gel-like substance that fills the interior of the cell. It houses various organelles and is where many cellular processes take place.

Nucleus:

The nucleus is the control center of the cell. It contains genetic material in the form of DNA, which carries instructions for cell functions and inheritance. The nucleus is surrounded by a nuclear membrane.

Nucleolus:

The nucleolus is found within the nucleus and is involved in the production of ribosomes, which are essential for protein synthesis.

Chloroplasts:

Chloroplasts are organelles unique to plant cells and some types of algae. They contain chlorophyll, a pigment that captures sunlight for photosynthesis, the process by which plants convert sunlight into energy and produce glucose.

Mitochondria:

Mitochondria are responsible for energy production through cellular respiration. They convert glucose and oxygen into ATP (adenosine triphosphate), the cell's energy currency.

Endoplasmic

Reticulum (ER): The endoplasmic reticulum is involved in protein synthesis and lipid metabolism. Rough ER is studded with ribosomes, while smooth ER lacks ribosomes.

Golgi Apparatus:

The Golgi apparatus modifies, sorts, and packages proteins and lipids produced by the endoplasmic reticulum for transport within the cell or secretion outside the cell.

Quiz questions

Fruit: 

1.What is the outermost layer of a fruit called?
2.Which part of the fruit contains the seeds?
3.What is the protective covering of a seed called?
4.In some fruits, what tissue surrounds and nourishes the embryo?
5.Which part of a fruit connects it to the plant?

Root:

1.What is the primary function of plant roots?
2.Which part of the root secretes lubricating substances?
3.Where does cell division occur in the root?
4.What is the outermost layer of root cells called?
5.Which region of the root gives rise to lateral roots?

Plant:

1.What are the primary functions of leaves in a plant?
2.What is the primary function of the stem?
3.Which part of the plant anchors it in the soil?
4.What tissue transports water and nutrients in a plant?
5.Where does cell division occur in both roots and shoots?

Cell:

1.What is the basic structural and functional unit of all living organisms?

2.Which part of the cell houses genetic material in the form of DNA?

3.What is the energy currency of a cell?

4.Which organelles are responsible for protein synthesis?

5.What is the term for the network of protein filaments that provides structural support in a cell?

Fruit

1. The outermost layer of a fruit is called the pericarp.
2. Seeds are typically found in the mesocarp or endocarp of the fruit.
3. The protective covering of a seed is called the seed coat or testa.
4. In some fruits, the tissue that surrounds and nourishes the embryo is ca called the endosperm.
5. The part of a fruit that connects it to the plant is the stem or peduncle.

Root

1. The primary function of plant roots is to absorb water and nutrients and anchor the plant.
2. The root cap secretes lubricating substances.
3. Cell division occurs in the meristem region of the root.
4. The outermost layer of root cells is called the epidermis.
5. The pericycle gives rise to lateral roots.

Plant:

1. Leaves in a plant primarily function in **photosynthesis,** capturing sunlight to produce energy.
2. The primary function of the stem is to **support the plant** and transport substances.
3. Roots anchor the plant in the soil.
4. **Xylem** and **phloem** tissues transport water and nutrients in a plant.
5. Cell division occurs in the **meristematic** tissues of both roots and shoots.

Cell

1. The basic structural and functional unit of all living organisms is the **cell.**
2. Genetic material in the form of DNA is housed in the **nucleus.**
3. The energy currency of a cell is **ATP (adenosine triphosphate).**
4. Organelles responsible for protein synthesis are **ribosomes.**
5. The network of protein filaments providing structural support in a cell is the **cytoskeleton.**

1.__________________

2.__________________

3.__________________

4.__________________

5.__________________

6.__________________

7.__________________

8.__________________

9.__________________

10.__________________

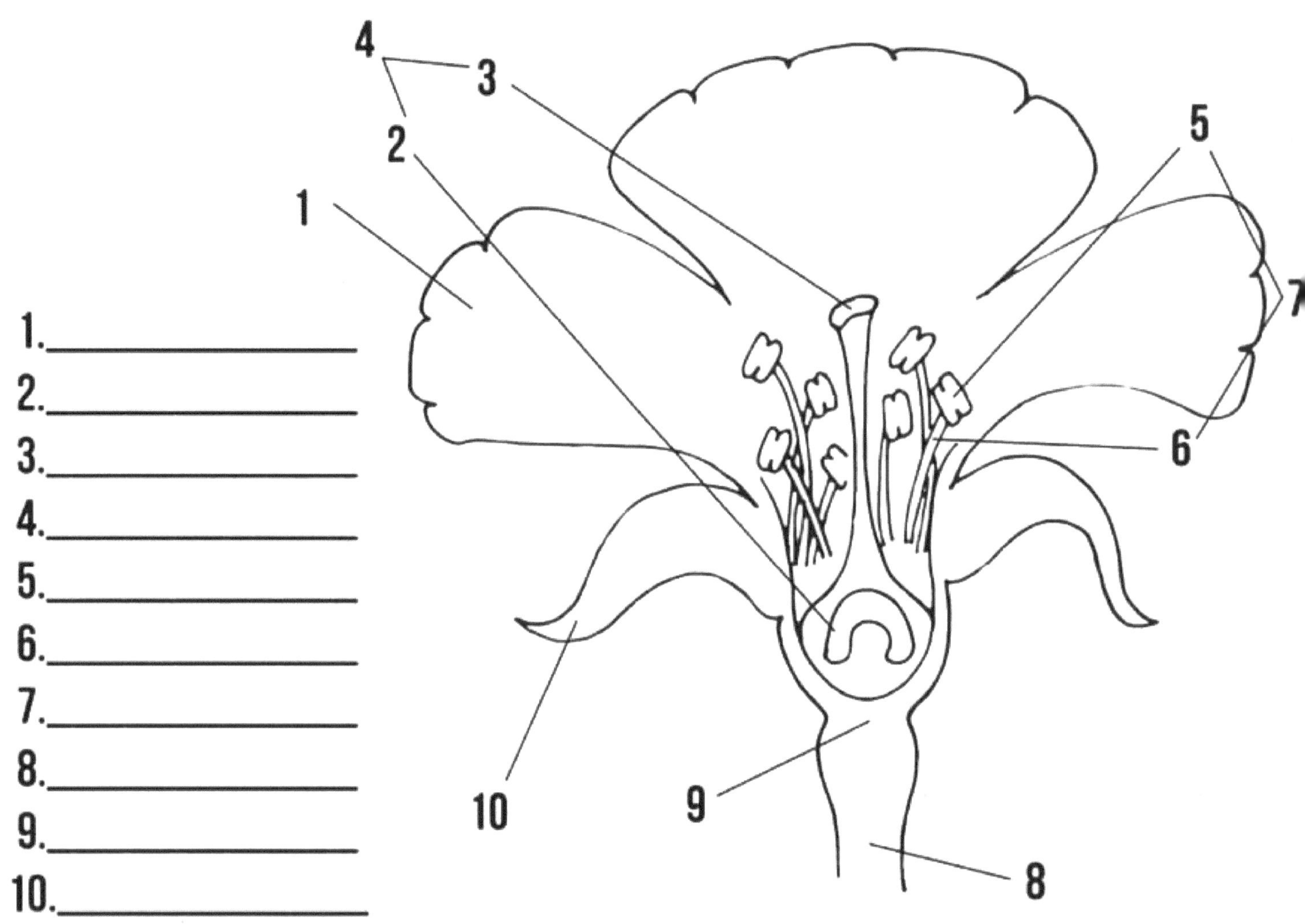

Fill-in-the-blank

1.Pollination is the transfer of _______ from the anther to the stigma.

2. The male part of a flower is called the _______.

3. The female part of a flower is called the _______.

4. In self-pollination, pollen moves to the stigma of the _______ flower or same plant.

5. Cross-pollination involves the transfer of pollen to a _______ plant.

6. Insect pollination is also called _______.

7. Bird pollination is known as _______.

8. Bat pollination happens mostly during the _______.

9. The part of the plant that absorbs water is the _______.

10. The root has tiny structures called _______ to absorb water.

11. The tip of the root is protected by the _______.

12. The life of a plant begins with a _______.

13. When a seed starts to grow, the process is called _______.

14. A young plant that grows from a seed is called a _______.

15. The process where flowers make seeds after pollination is called _______.

16. Wind-pollinated plants produce a lot of _______.

17. _______ is the type of pollination where pollen floats on water.

18. The stage in a plant's life cycle where it has flowers is called the _______ plant stage.

19. Seeds are often spread by animals, wind, or _______.

20. The green part of the plant that makes food is the _______.

Answers

1. pollen
2. stamen
3. pistil
4. same
5. different
6. entomophily
7. ornithophily
8. night
9. root
10. root hairs
11. root cap
12. seed
13. germination
14. seedling
15. fertilization
16. pollen
17. hydrophily
18. adult
19. water
20. leaf

www.ingramcontent.com/pod-product-compliance
Lightning Source LLC
Chambersburg PA
CBHW040201240726

48664CB00002B/794